Walter's Theory

By
Jay Lillibridge

Dedication

iii

I would like to dedicate this book to Walter, one of the wisest men I have ever met.

Table of Contents

Chapter 1:
New Year's at the Mansion

In mid-December of 1999, my wife Theresa and I received a very flattering invitation to a New Year's Eve party at a newly acquired mansion. The estate had been purchased by a family that had enjoyed considerable success in business over the years. The invitation was flattering because I had always lived paycheck to paycheck. Because quite frankly, I was broke, and so were most of my friends. I didn't really know our hosts that well, but my wife had been friends with their daughter-in-law for a number of years when they were both broke.

Kristy married into a wealthy family, and we had attended their wedding. That had been a very lavish affair, so we were sure that the New Year's Eve party would be a special event. I was also hopeful that I would not find myself at home fighting to stay awake in front of the television, waiting for Dick Clark to count down the final seconds as the big ball in Time Square made its traditional descent. I had long since given up having New Year's Eve parties because of a series of abysmal failures.

Most of my friends know me, but they don't know each other. It's very difficult to keep a group of strangers entertained until midnight when you are the only thing they have in common. My last party was so bad that I vowed never to have another one.

Of the 15 couples we invited to attend, only two came, and one of them left at 10:00 PM to attend another party. I really wish I could have left with them. The highlight of the evening was emptying the 30 cans of "Silly String" in a half-hearted battle at midnight. Our guests left at 12:07 AM, and I felt like a failure for the next eleven and a half months.

Given my pathetic history with New Year's Eve parties, you can imagine how excited I was to attend a New Year's Eve party at a "Mansion" full of wealthy, interesting people.

Undaunted by the "formal attire only" notice at the bottom of the page, I bolted out the door to rent the coolest tux I could find.

I passed by the powder blue model that had looked so cool when I chose it for my wedding in the seventies and settled on a sophisticated black number that shouted, "I'm a big-boy now!"

I even gave Theresa a carte blanch to purchase a new dress just for the occasion, which turned out to be a mistake as she spent a lot of money on a dress that I really didn't like.

The magic night arrived, and we pulled our car into the circular driveway of the large brick Tudor mansion. I want to stress here that I am not totally materialistic, but I do appreciate well-landscaped grounds and classic architecture.

By any standard, this house was a classic. I guessed that it had been built in the 1920s by some high-flying investor anxious to impress the blue bloods with old money. I was fantasizing about my "high flier" jumping out a window in 1929 when the sound of the doorbell brought me back to the present. We were warmly greeted by Theresa's friend Kristy, who escorted us into a large parlor with high ceilings and several tables of exotic delicacies.

We spent the early part of the evening meeting various members of Hanna's family and a variety of friends. It was a very diverse gathering, especially in terms of the age groups represented. There were babies, teenagers, young adults, mature adults, and very mature adults. I mingled with the group, wondering to myself exactly how our host had become wealthy enough to purchase "The Mansion."

After several hours of meeting and greeting people, I met Walter. A kindly gentleman in his mid-70s, Walter had that sparkle in his eyes that belied a keen mind and a love of people. Early into our conversation, I learned that Walter had been a business partner of our host for many years. It seems that they held seminars aimed at securing investment clients. I was so impressed with Walter that I could have talked with him all night.

He was fiercely intelligent, but he had a warmth that radiated right through me. I felt like we really connected, but I also realized that Walter probably could connect easily with a wide variety of people. When he asked me what I did for a living, I announced proudly that I sold surgical instruments to doctors. He smiled and asked me a question that changed my life.

"What do you think is the most important reason why a customer would prefer to do business with one salesperson over another?"

I thought it over for a few minutes and said, "It's a matter of genuine concern for the customers' needs. A good sales person listens to his customers, discovers needs, and then meets those needs with the right product."

Walter just looked at me and smiled as he said, "That's a very good answer, but that's not THE answer."

"Integrity!" I blurted out, certain that this could not be far from the answer.

"No," Walter replied with the warmest of smiles.

"Personality," I chirped, "the salesman with the best personality and professional manner will usually win the customer's loyalty."

Walter started laughing at my enthusiasm, but the answer was still "No."

"The favored salesperson is the better listener?"

"No."

"Trust," I said, "it has to be a matter of trust!"

Walter just continued to smile and shook his head slowly, side to side.

"The customer simply likes one sales person more than another."

At this, Walter said, "Yes, of course, he does, and people will do as much business as they can with people they like and as little business as they can with people they don't like. But the real question is, 'Why do they like one salesperson more than another?'"

"The customer prefers to work with the salesperson who is the best dressed?"

"Has the gift of gab?" I was really grasping at straws now, but THE answer continued to elude me.

So, I ask you now, what would your answer be? Why does someone prefer to do business with one person over another? What is the most important factor?

Before I tell you what Walter revealed to me, I should warn you that I have asked this question hundreds of times over the past 24 years, and NOT ONCE has anyone given me what I am now convinced is THE correct answer.

Walter lowered his voice and slowly whispered, **"The main reason a client prefers to do business with a certain salesperson is that the client perceives that the salesperson thinks he is COMPETENT in his position."**

I was stunned and a little confused. "Are you saying that if I make a sales call and the person that I call on thinks that I think he's good at his job, he's more likely to do business with me?"

"That's exactly right!" Walter shouted.

"So, if I think that the person that I'm addressing is COMPETENT, he is going to want to do business with me as opposed to my competitors."

"That's it!" Walter beamed.

All I could say was, "Wow," as the implications of Walter's suggestion tumbled through my consciousness. My mind was in high gear. I was trying to think of all the people that had been easy for me to do business with—Ron, the materials manager at St. Agnes Medical Center, for example.

We had always had a special connection. It wasn't that he didn't challenge me because he certainly did.

But I thought he was very competent! I respected Ron because he never left any money on the table during our negotiations. He did a good job for his hospital. So, I had to admit that at least as far as my relationship with Ron was concerned, it seemed to fit *Walter's Theory.*

Quickly, my mind moved to the negative side of the equation, and I began to consider people to whom I had difficulty selling Chiclets. In particular, Barbara at Mass General came to mind. She had promised me business on more than one occasion only to withdraw the opportunity at a later date. I definitely thought she was incompetent and unprofessional.

"Well, she was incompetent and unprofessional," I told myself under my breath.

So, what good did that assessment do me? It led to so much acrimony that I couldn't sell free foot rubs in her hospital for over 22 years. This is kind of surprising because she left the hospital after only 10 years. I would hate to try and place a dollar value on the cost of this failed relationship.

Walter's Theory regarding the importance of competence continued to bounce around in my mind for the next several years. During that time, I have asked hundreds of sales professionals, managers, and friends the same question Walter asked me. The fact that no one came close to THE answer continues to fascinate me! It seemed that

Walter's Theory of the Perception of Competence was a previously unknown concept. I made up my mind that night to test the theory in the crucible of experience.

Chapter 2:
Defining Competence and
Incompetence

Since the term competent and the concept of competency are so central and unique to *Walter's Theory*, it's important to examine the meaning of the word. It may seem a little simplistic, but it's essential if *Walter's Theory* is to be proven.

The first dictionary I consulted defined competent as ***well qualified, capable, fit, possessing ability, and sufficient means for one's needs.***

I decided to look up all the related words from this definition as well as previously unmentioned words that appeared in those definitions. Here are the results of the resulting "definition tree:"

Qualified—Fit for an office or occupation. Having the necessary or desirable qualities. Having met the conditions or requirements set.

Capable—Having ability, able to do things well, skilled.

Fit—To be suitably adapted, suited to some purpose or function. Adapted, adjusted, qualified, or suited to some purpose, function, or situation.

Skilled—Having or requiring an ability as in a particular industrial occupation, gained by special experience or training.

Skill—Great ability or proficiency, expertise that comes from training and practice.

Ability—The power to do something physical or mental. Expertness or talent.

Proficient—Highly **_competent,_** skilled, adept, and has expertise.

Adept—Highly skilled expert. Alchemists claiming to have arrived at the Philosopher's Stone.

Expert—Very skillful, a person who is very skillful or highly trained and informed in some special field. Able, adept, finished, masterly, polished, efficient.

Efficient—Capable, able, effective, causing effects, producing results.

Reading all these definitions, we began to get a more complete picture of the overwhelmingly positive nature of this term. What human being would not want to be described as capable, able, effective, adept, proficient, expert, skilled, fit, qualified, and competent?

Of course, the opposite corollary to *Walter's Theory* is also worth considering. How could any human being tolerate being considered *incapable, unable, ineffective, novice, inept, inefficient, unskilled, unfit, unqualified and incompetent?*

Truly, these terms were overwhelmingly negative, and attributing them to an individual would surely have a negative effect. So, if competence is such a powerful positive term and incompetence is such a powerful negative term, why hasn't anyone I've interviewed over the years considered perceived competence as an important factor in the nature of relationships? I think it's because we don't believe that people are mind readers. We mistakenly believe that our attitude, our habitual pattern of thought about another person, is our little secret.

The truth is that people can read our minds, and they know exactly what we think about them regardless of what we say to their faces. Consider the estimates that 70 to 90% of communication is non-verbal. If we think that the person we are talking to is incompetent, our polite words, compliments, and flattery will be a whisper compared to the non-verbal shouting that screams our true feelings at them. If you go into a meeting with someone that you think is incompetent, you might as well have a flashing neon sign on your forehead broadcasting your belief **because they will perceive it!**

You may not agree with me on this, and since I have yet to prove it, I'd like to call this concept **Roger's Corollary** in honor of my recently departed father. (Roger's my first name also, so I can honor my father and share in the name.)

Roger's Corollary postulates that in any face-to-face meeting between two people, the true attitudes of each will be perceived by the other.

I realize that, on the surface, this does not seem possible because it does not explain how some people are able to deceive others. It's important to note that we often ignore our perceptions about someone and allow ourselves to be deceived. So, the ability of someone to tell a lie and have another person believe it does not invalidate Roger's Corollary.

On some level, the person being deceived knows that they are being deceived, but they discount the perception for some other reason, such as greed. This is the principle that all con artists count on. That greed will blind the "mark" to ignore his perception of the con artist and the situation. Roger's Corollary holds that we know on some level when we are being lied to, but we often choose to ignore our perception because we want to believe the lie for some reason.

Consider some of our prominent politicians. I can think of more than one politician who lied to the voters numerous times before he was elected, who told more whoppers after he was elected, and who was then re-elected. A majority of people simply ignored their perceptions of this man because they wanted to believe that he cared about them, and they were anxious to receive the things that he promised to give them.

Chapter 3:
Good Boss, Bad Boss

When I first graduated from college, I really didn't know what I wanted to do with my life, but I hoped that there would be a significant amount of financial compensation involved. I loved airplanes as a child, so when people asked me that time-honored question for kids, "What do you want to be when you grow up?"

I always said that I wanted to be an aeronautical engineer. It sounded really impressive, but I was 18 years old before I realized exactly what an aeronautical engineer does. I also realized at the same time that just because I had been good at building Revell model airplanes, there were no guarantees that I had the talent necessary to be good at designing the real thing.

In fact, I had none of the skills essential for success as an engineer of any kind. For one thing, I could draw a straight line with a t-square. I had no concept of design and no spatial creativity, but I could talk, so… I moved from my aeronautical engineer phase to my lawyer phase. I was convinced from watching Raymond Burr's portrayal of Perry Mason on television that being a successful lawyer was the way to go. Nobody messed with Perry Mason!

The idea of defeating the "Mr. Bergers" of the world had a very strong romantic appeal, and I was pretty sure that I did have the skills to be successful. I took the LSAT exams as a sophomore for practice and passed them with a high enough score to apply to law school.

Unfortunately, I soon learned that I had absolutely no aptitude for law. In my first law course as a junior, my weakness surfaced! I picked the wrong party to prevail in about 90% of the cases I read. Clearly, I wasn't going to be the next Perry Mason.

After my brief and discouraging lawyer phase, I moved on to my just get a degree and get a job phase. Eventually, I graduated with a degree in economics, but I really didn't have any interest in being an economist. I landed a job with Dumpster's Department Store after graduation as an assistant buyer/management trainee. They told me that if I did well, I could expect to be promoted to the buyer in 5 to 7 years.

Eighteen months later, I became a buyer of skiwear, swimwear, and athletic wear. My boss in this new position was a young phoneme named Alex Fastrack. He was only a few years older than I was, but he had already made the leap from buyer to divisional manager. Alex was a great boss. He was intelligent, hard-working, and creative, and he was literally on a fast track to the top of the organization. What I loved about working for Alex was the lack of ambiguity. We met frequently in his office to discuss various issues. When I presented Alex with a problem, it was never without also offering up three or four potential solutions.

After listening carefully, he would always either choose one of my options, or he would substitute one of his own. When I walked out of his office a few minutes later, the course of action had been settled. I would do my part to execute the plan, and he would support me 100%. It was not always an easy job, but working with Alex was very satisfying. We were a successful team. We didn't become friends, and I was very careful not to become a flattering, brown-nosing sycophant. I did respect Alex, and I did think he was extremely competent.

The department I took over had been the store's biggest loser over the past two years. It was so bad that my predecessor had been fired despite his long tenure with the company. On our first buying tip together, Alex asked me what we needed to do to turn things around. I told him we needed to keep jogging suits from a certain vendor in stock. I knew they were a hot item, and the previous buyer had never had sufficient quantities on hand. Alex trusted me.

The next day, we met with the jogging suit manufacturer, and Alex committed the money to buy their entire remaining inventory and challenged them to kccp us well supplied in the months ahead.

When the product came in, we filled the previously empty department with jogging suits and ran a few ads. Sales skyrocketed, and soon, we were carrying jogging suits from five different manufacturers in a variety of styles and price points—twenty-three years old, 18 months on the job, and I was the hero!

Six months after I became the buyer of a very small department, they gave me responsibility for two additional departments, quadrupling my volume and doubling my starting salary. I really thought I was going to be the store's youngest vice president in a few short years. It was a heady experience. I've since learned that the expression "heady experience." Meaning that the experience can cause you to lose your head, and that's exactly what happened to me. I just assumed that I could follow Alex right to the top. The great thing about it was that I hadn't resorted to "kissing up" in order to succeed.

Then, my circumstances changed dramatically. Success is a fickle mistress, and I was about to learn a painful but enduring lesson. Alex was promoted to vice president of merchandising for ladies' sportswear. At first, I thought this would be a positive change. My mentor now held a higher position in the company, which I assumed would bode well for my future.

Well, you know the old adage about how things turn out when you "assume" too much. To replace Alex, the president of the company, Dick Kissupski, brought in Oscar Moran, an old crony and tennis buddy from his previous posting in the Midwest.

My first impression of Oscar was very positive. He was a fit, athletic man in his early 40s with a firm handshake and an easy, broad smile. His passion was tennis. He played every weekend with Dick, and I came to suspect he knew how and when to lose. He was, in fact, "a nice guy" and a good loser.

It didn't take me long to conclude, however, that Vince Lombardi was right when he said, "Show me a 'good loser,' and I'll show you a loser."

During the previous two years, when Dick Kissupski was the vice president, I had quickly concluded that he was a classic brown noser who had kissed up and coat-tailed his way to the top. This belief was strangely confirmed by a full-page color print that appeared in a magazine just before Dick was promoted. The picture showed a number of men in business suits on hands and knees at various elevations on a large, smooth mountain.

They were all kissing the surface of the mountain, which you realized upon closer examination was a giant gluteus maximus. The amazing thing about the picture was that the business man nearest the top looked just exactly like our own Dick Kissupski. I thought this was so funny that I immediately cut out the picture and pinned it on the wall in my office.

The joke was on me, though, because Oscar Moran had been brought all the way from Indiana to take Dick's place on the mountain because Dick had become the mountain.

On our first buying trip to New York, Oscar and I got along very well. He was positive and passionate about his new position, and he had no doubt been told about our recent success. I had no reason to suspect that my star would not continue to rise under Oscar's management. After all, Alex was Oscar's boss, and I was Alex's diamond in the rough.

Over the next six months, I became very disillusioned with Oscar. He was the anti-Alex. When I walked into my private meetings with Oscar, I tried to follow the same protocol that had worked so well under Alex. I would present the facts to define the problem I was facing, along with several options for a course of action.

Unfortunately, Oscar did not have the courage to make a decision. The decision was left in my hands. If the decision I made turned out well, Oscar would accept praise for a job well done from his superiors. If the results were negative, he would blame me for making a poor decision. I began to see Oscar as a coward incapable of supporting his subordinates. He simply would not back me up on anything that didn't turn out well. Where Alex had been strong and decisive, Oscar was weak and double-minded.

The result was a work environment similar to a Dilbert strip.

Every day was filled with ambiguity and paradox. I was miserable working for this "Oscar-moron!" I started complaining to the other buyers during coffee and lunch breaks that Oscar was an idiot. I could not believe that this man had been in retailing for over 20 years and that he had learned so little. I didn't realize how adept he was at "kissing the mountain" because I was young, arrogant, and naive. I thought you could rise to the top by simply doing your job well.

There is one particular incident that illustrates my frustration in dealing with Oscar. Each month, all buyers were required to submit a "markdown budget." This written request was supposed to include the total dollars that you planned to use to "mark down" items during sales and promotions planned for the upcoming month.

For example, if you planned to have a 20% off sale on a group of winter coats and the total retail value of the inventory equaled $10,000. Then, you were required to submit a request for $2,000 in markdown money. Requests were then approved by your boss and his boss. Once the request was approved, the buyer was expected to finish the month within the budget. This probably sounds very simple, and it should have been, but with an Oscar-moron at the hclm, steering the ship was never simple.

It was mid-November, and I was preparing to turn in my markdown budget for December. By the way, if anyone reading this story works in the retail industry, you have my total respect and sympathy for what you must endure during the Christmas season. To tell the truth, working in a department store at Christmas totally exposes you to the darker side of human nature.

In this instance, my nightmare began when Oscar called me into his office for a private meeting to discuss my December markdown budget. I had requested $33,000 in markdown money to cover our big holiday sale. We planned to advertise a large group of wool coordinates from a popular manufacturer.

I estimated that we would have about $100,000 worth of merchandise by the date of the sale, and the established price point for this type of group was 1/3 off. Oscar appeared agitated when I entered the office, so I instinctively closed the door behind me to avoid involving the secretaries in my nightmare.

As soon as I sat down, Oscar shoved a piece of paper across the satin top of his mahogany desk at me. The paper was stiff, and it had enough thrust behind it to float over the edge of the desk and flutter into my lap.

"That's your December markdown budget," he declared as he peered over the top of his thick glasses.

I picked up the paper and felt instantly dizzy and nauseous. My heart started pounding in the face of a battle that I knew I could not win or even fight. ***This had to be a joke!***

Then, I remembered that Oscar did not have a sense of humor. The paper was my original request for $33,000 in markdowns. At the bottom of the page, the figure $33,000 was crossed out in red ink, and the figure $6,000 appeared in its place. This number was underlined and followed by three large red exclamation points. If I had been standing, I'm pretty sure I would have fainted.

I tried to compose myself. In slow, measured tones, I said, "Oscar, it's going to take more than this to mark down the holiday wool group we're running."

Please, let there be some hint of a possible misunderstanding here.

"That's what you have to work with!" He shot back as though the answer was a bullet already chambered and ready to fire before the question was asked.

"Alright, then, I guess that means we'll be postponing the 1/3 off sale on the holiday wool group until January."

Of course, that's what it has to mean because simple math takes over now, right? Right, Oscar?

"No way!" he shouted. "We need that group in the December holiday sale."

You just don't get it, do ya, kid?

"I agree, but it's going to take $33,000 in markdown money to reduce the price of the wool group to 1/3 off for the December Sale."

I was beginning to panic because this was a dead end, and I was trapped. So many of my "problem-solving sessions" with Oscar had gone like this, and none of them had ever been resolved satisfactorily.

How could this man be so dense as to deny the basic mathematics of the situation?

"You have $6,000, and that's all you're going to get!" he boomed. I noticed veins and eyeballs bulging with the force of his declaration, and I knew the end of our discussion was near.

"Oscar, with $6,000, I can mark the group down to 6% off. Is that what you'd like me to do?" I had decided at this point that I had nothing to lose by giving him another option that fit the budget.

Maybe this time, he will see that he is asking me to do something that is mathematically impossible.

His face reddened and threw me a line I didn't expect.

"I know you think I'm an 'idiot,'" he countered, shocking me so much that it took all my willpower not to nod my head in the affirmative, "but what you think of me doesn't matter. I expect you to just do your job."

I made one last desperate attempt to reconcile the Oscar-moron. "Oscar, how can I mark down $100,000 worth of merchandise to 1/3 off with only $6,000 in markdown money?"

Oscar just smiled like the cat that swallowed the canary and crooned, "That's your problem."

Then, he broke off eye contact and began shuffling through the papers from his "In" box, signifying that the audience was over: game, set, and match.

I stumbled upstairs, grabbing one of my fellow buyers along the way for solace. I relayed the details of the latest chapter in the continuing saga, "Oscar Is an Idiot," in hopes of lessening my pain.

"By the way, Keith, you didn't happen to tell anyone that I think Oscar's an idiot, did you?"

Maybe, despite all his faults, Oscar had some insight into my thoughts about him.

As I began to consider the paradox that I faced, the thing that bothered me most was that I sensed that Oscar expected me to cook the books expertly enough to avoid detection in order to accomplish the impossible and mark down the group and still stay within the budget.

The final "that's your problem" made it pretty clear that he expected this. I'm now convinced that the unwavering inflexibility of simple mathematics in situations like this is at the core of all major corporate scandals. I really had only two choices.

First, I could follow the implied directive to "cheat" and take $33,000 in markdowns while reporting only $6,000. This course of action would require an elaborate scheme to cover up the shortage in valuation before January's upcoming physical inventory.

Second, I could simply take the markdowns honestly and take the heat after the fact. I called this the "damn the torpedoes, full speed ahead" strategy in honor of my favorite naval commander, David Farragut.

After a number of sleepless nights, I committed to this option. It was definitely the more romantic of the two, and I still believed that I was an honest person. On December 31, I turned in the written markdowns for December totaling $34,569.13 and headed home to host another pathetic "New Year's Eve Party."

When I walked into my office on Monday, January 3, there was a stack of messages from Oscar's secretary, Lois. Instantly, the hairs stood up on the back of my neck. I knew that this was going to be ugly. I called Lois, and she informed me in the most pleasant voice that Oscar wanted to see me as soon as possible. I wanted to run away, to somehow escape the inevitable, but there was nowhere to run and nowhere to hide. The subsequent meeting was worse than I feared. Oscar was furious. I was his target. Bloody Monday had arrived with a vengeance.

"What the hell is this?" he shouted as he flipped paper across the desk at me.

"It's my December markdowns, Oscar," I replied timidly.

I really don't like being yelled at by people twice my age and twice my size. Can't we just discuss this calmly? Did you really expect me to "cook the books" so you could look good on paper?

Oscar's face looked like it was going to hemorrhage.

"This is more than $28,000 over your **approved** budget! What the hell did you think you were doing?"

I'd like to say that I was calm and cool under pressure, but the truth is that I was a scared twenty-four-year-old kid sweating bullets. That old cliché kids use, ***"sticks and stones may break my bones,*** *but words can never hurt me,"* couldn't be further from the truth. Words can do a lot more damage than sticks and stones.

Finally, after letting the sting of Oscar's attack subside a little, I meekly squeaked, "I marked down the holiday wool group to 1/3 off for sale."

All Oscar could say was, "This is totally unacceptable! Don't ever let anything like this happen again!"

I knew the meeting was over. "Would you like me to leave your door open?"

I asked this question in hopes of defusing the situation just a little as I got up to leave.

"No!"

My olive branch rejected, I slid out the door with what was left of my chewed tail tucked between my legs and gently closed the door as though a baby were asleep in the office. I went back to my little Dilbert Cubicle with the heat and water pipes running through it and tried to put Oscar's tirade out of my mind. I didn't really get much done the rest of the day. Even coffee with my peers, Wayne, Linda, and Keith, didn't offer much solace this time.

On the way home, I played the radio loud to take my mind off Oscar's impossible rhetorical questions. I couldn't help but smile when they played *Monday,*

Monday **by the Mamas and Papas. What a stupid name for a singing group!**

I started singing along to the chorus, modifying the words slightly:

> **But Monday morning**
>
> **You gave me no warning of what was to be…**
>
> **That Monday evening, you would take a bite out of me!**
>
> **Every other day, every other day of the week is fine…**
>
> **Ya, but when Bloody Monday comes,**
>
> **But when Bloody Monday comes…**
>
> **You can find me cryin' in the soup line!**

I really couldn't sleep that night, wondering if Tuesday could somehow be worse. I was really beginning to hate the job I had loved just a few months earlier.

About a month later, I was called into Dick Kissupski's office for my semi-annual performance review. Despite all the difficulties I had experienced with Oscar Moran during the previous year, I had increased the bottom-line profit margin in my departments by over $250,000.

Statistically, I knew that this was one of the top performances in the organization, and I was looking forward to a raise. Silly me. I was about to learn another painful lesson in corporate politics!

I sat outside Dick's office for about 20 minutes, waiting my turn before the trio of managers who would determine how much I would be paid for the coming year. I had a computer copy of my department's stellar financial results for the previous year in my lap, which I glanced at every few seconds for comfort. It had been a very good year, and I was looking forward to going over the numbers with my superiors. Finally, the large door opened, and Chuck Peterson, one of my fellow buyers, stepped out with a controlled smile on his face.

I stood and moved through the open door and took the only open seat in the room. To my left was Alex Fasttrack; behind the large desk in the center sat Dick Kissupski, and to my immediate right was Oscar Moran. My chair was a small, straight-backed style positioned with the back against the wall near the door. Oscar began the review with a negative appraisal of my attitude, which he described as "not very team-oriented."

He continued in this vein for what seemed like an eternity. Finally, there was a brief mention of the statistical performance being "satisfactory," followed by a further comment about the need to improve my "attitude." I was asked if I had any questions.

When I said I didn't, I was shown the door. I left the room totally deflated and stunned. I had no idea what it meant to have a "bad attitude." I have since found a definition that seems to fit. Your "attitude" is your habitual pattern of thought. Most of my thoughts about Oscar were negative, so I realized that that's what he had focused on.

After the review, I realized that nothing had been said about any increase in my salary. After all, I had increased the bottom-line profit of the department by over $250,000, which I thought was pretty good for a kid on a salary of

$14,500 per year.

At the first opportunity, I asked Alex about my annual raise. His reply doubled me over like a punch in the gut, "After a review like that, did you really expect a raise?"

I couldn't say anything. I just looked at him with that dumb-struck look of total surprise.

Yes, I really did think I was going to get a raise despite having a "bad attitude." This is a business where you hound me about the numbers on a daily basis. Now, you say the numbers don't matter as much as the fact that I think my boss is an idiot.

Shouldn't I get a bigger raise to increase the store's profit in spite of the fact that my boss is an idiot?

I turned and walked back to my little cubby office with the heating and plumbing pipes running overhead. It really pained me to realize that I was a bigger idiot than Oscar Moran! At least he knew how to keep his footing on the mountain. I, on the other hand, had created my own personal avalanche and then been buried by it.

A few months later, I walked into Oscar's office and handed him my resignation. He simply smiled. He had won! I had lost. I would never replace him. Political savvy and experience had triumphed over youth and talent!

I spent the next two weeks sitting by the pool in my apartment complex, trying to understand where it all went wrong at Dumpster's. Now I realize that the experience I had serves to validate *Walter's Theory*. I had considered Alex Fasttrack to be a very competent person, and my relationship with him was a very successful partnership.

On the other hand, I had considered Oscar to be totally incompetent, and our relationship was a disaster. While these two relationships weren't enough to prove that *Walter's Theory* is correct, they do offer sufficient evidence to continue the examination of other relationships.

I also want to point out that many of the problems that I had with Oscar were made more severe by my youth, arrogance, inexperience, pride, and self-centered perspective. I've often wondered how much different things could have been if I had known about ***Walter's Theory.*** Perhaps I could have applied the principles to my advantage.

Chapter 4:
Reaching the Unreachable

I wasn't completely reckless when I quit my job at Dumpster's Department Store. I had secured a job with the Schlocky Stock Stores the day before I walked into Oscar Moran's office and handed him my resignation. Schlocky Stock Stores had a reputation for selling off-brand clothing at lower prices than Dumpster's and Nordstrom, and they had a large number of stores.

They were also the only people I talked to who were interested in giving me a job. Schlocky Stock was the only escape route available to me on short notice, so I took the position as an assistant store manager with a reduced salary. I would have to prove myself before I would be considered for a position as a buyer.

My first assignment was in Gotham, a small suburban community outside the city limits. The store was brand new. I reported to Rich Kingman, the store manager, on a sunny summer morning, and I was immediately treated to breakfast at the café within the store. I liked Rich immediately! He was a wiry, high-energy guy with a good sense of humor and a positive attitude. It took me less than an hour to decide that I would be much happier working for

Rich at Schlocky Stock's Gotham Store than I had been working for Oscar Moran at Dumpster's.

Rich was very positive and encouraging in his interactions with me. I don't ever remember him saying anything critical or negative about my work. I respected him immensely. There is no doubt that I viewed him as extremely organized, capable, competent, and skilled.

As a result, our working relationship was fantastic. We were a very productive team, and the fifty employees who reported to us responded accordingly. The store was a showplace for Schlocky Stock, as evidenced by the constant flow of senior managers and potential investors who toured the facility. My creative energy and self-confidence were quickly restored as I prepared to succeed with Schlocky Stock.

After only 3 months with Rich Kingman, I received word from Doris Sharky, the regional manager, that I was being transferred to the Howling St. Store for further training. Every store within the Schlocky chain had its own personality and reputation. The Howling Street Store was notorious as one of the worst stores in the chain. Rich assured me that my transfer to Howling St. was a sign that Doris held me in high regard. Bad stores like Howling Street were considered crucibles where talented young managers could prove their worth.

Howling Street was located in a neighborhood populated with drug dealers, their doper clients, prostitutes, thieves, and the mentally ill. The store itself was old, dingy, and foreboding. The main feature was a concrete ramp that ran from the parking lot to the roof of the store, where an additional parking lot was located. I often wondered what the architect had hoped to achieve by putting a concrete parking lot on top of a one-level store.

Every day, I expected cars and minivans to fall through the ceiling into my little Schlocky Stock department. You could almost feel the weight of the parked cars on your shoulders at various times during the day. The paint peeling off of the exposed pipes that ran along the high dusty ceilings only added to the dismal atmosphere of the place.

The store manager I reported to was Jim Sluggard. Jim was in his early forties, and he clearly felt the job was beneath him. He grunted most of his orders to me in horror movie dialogue. Nearly all our communication was a grunt in response to a question from me.

"Jim, would you like me to do this week's schedule today?" I asked.

"Sgrrrrrrr (Jim's word for 'sure, son, go right ahead')."

"How are store sales trending this year?" I ventured.

"Gownnnn." He groaned (sales were down, of course).

"Were there any special projects you'd like me to focus on this week, Jim?"

"NO!" he snapped. At least this last word was clear and intelligible!

Over the next few weeks, it became clear that my main purpose was to act as a buffer between Jim and the thirty-five women who made up our staff. They were quite an interesting group. Several of our older "ladies" had been working in this store for over 20 years. Perhaps one-third of them had been around for at least 10 years. Jim told me that they had seen a lot of hot-shot assistant managers come and go over the years. The message was very clear!

No matter what I said or did, this stuff was going to plod along at the same leisurely pace they had maintained for decades. They were "unreachable," and if I thought I could affect any positive changes in them, I was deluding myself.

Despite Jim's gloomy assessment, I spent the next several weeks trying to prove him wrong. It was very depressing work, and I soon began to believe that maybe Jim had been right. I continued to interact with each "lady" like a bee buzzing from one flower to the next while Jim stood behind his beloved counter/desk at one end of the department with a bemused smirk on his face that shouted, "I told you so!"

Things had settled into a boring routine by the end of the summer when a large bundle wrapped in brown paper arrived at the store addressed to Jim Sluggard, store manager. My curiosity was heightened by my growing boredom with the mundane and repetitive nature of my job, but Jim just pushed the package aside as if he already knew its contents.

"Jim, that package looks important. Aren't you going to open it?" I asked.

"Don't need to, yet!" Good ol' Jim, never one to waste words.

Hoping to spur his curiosity, I pressed on, "Do you know what it is?"

"Yep." More brevity from the master.

"Well, what is it?" I wasn't going to let this go, and I think Jim began to realize it.

"It's the packet for 'White Glove,' kid—no need to do anything with it now. 'White Glove' isn't until November this year."

With that declaration, Jim took the brown paper bundle and buried it on a lower-level shelf in his stand-up desk/counter fortress, where it remained unopened for the next two months.

About once a week, I'd ask Jim about that 'White Glove' thing, but I never got more than a dismissive grunt in response. The "ladies" added to my apprehension by answering my questions about 'White Glove' with a "deer in the headlights" gaze and a few mumbled words about a lot of work.

Finally, the situation became startlingly clear on a cold Friday morning in mid-November.

Doris Sharkey, the regional manager, came into the Howling Street Store at about 8:30 AM and asked Jim Sluggard to join her for coffee. At precisely 8:37 AM, Doris returned and asked me to join her for coffee. I liked Doris, but I was also a little afraid of her. She had to be in her late sixties, but one look in her steely-grey eyes told you that this lady was a serious businesswoman.

As we sat down that chilly morning, Doris got right to the point. "Jim is leaving us, and we'd like you to take over as acting manager for the balance of the year."

It was hard to contain my excitement. I was going to have the opportunity to manage the store after only a few months' tenure with Schlocky Stock.

"This will be a very critical time for the Howling St. Store," Doris continued. "There's the 'White Glove

Inspection' in two weeks, followed by the Christmas Peak and the inventory in January. I've watched you over the past few months, and I believe that you can handle this."

Now, I was both scared and excited as my mind jumped from one possibility to the next.

Then, Doris asked the question I had been dreading. "Now, tell me what preparations you have made for 'White Glove?'"

I'm a firm believer that honesty is almost always the best policy, so I replied, "Doris, we haven't done anything to prepare, and I'm not even sure what 'White Glove' is."

Doris blinked like she'd been splashed in the face with ice water, but she quickly regained her balance. "Haven't you seen the mailing that was sent out in August?"

"I saw something, but Jim put it away and told me not to worry about it?"

Doris was composed again. "You'll need to open that up, read it thoroughly, and then let me know how many additional staff hours you're going to need to get ready. I'll approve as much as I can. You're already nine weeks behind in preparation, but just do the best you can."

I could tell that the meeting was almost over, so I

asked Doris the one question at the top of my mind. "Doris, I'm grateful for this opportunity, and I appreciate the confidence you have shown in me, but I couldn't help but notice that no mention was made of any change in my compensation."

This question drew a stern scolding look from Doris Sharky. It was almost as though any raise in my pay would be coming out of her pocket. Her reply was swift and cold. "We'll evaluate your performance and consider adjusting your compensation in January. You've only been with us for four months."

The realization that I was going to take on a lot more work without any raise in my pay didn't sit well with me. "So, what you're saying is that you believe that I can handle the additional responsibility, but you're not sure I can handle any additional compensation."

While this may have been true, Doris Sharky didn't appreciate me pointing it out to her. "We'll discuss this again in January. In the meantime, I suggest you read through your 'White Glove' packet."

I thanked Doris again and jogged to the manager's desk/counter fortress to delve into the 'White Glove' mystery. I reached down to the bottom shelf where Jim had hidden the instructions, and I ripped open the brown paper wrapping. I couldn't help but think about those advertisements for something that might prove embarrassing.

The ads always promise to ship your purchase in an unmarked brown paper wrapper so your neighbors wouldn't know that you were dumb enough to order the latest snake oil cure for baldness, obesity, memory loss, arthritis, old age, or the malady of the month. The package was the size of standard 8 ½ by 11-inch paper and about 6 inches high.

Inside were detailed instructions for the cleaning, organization, and presentation of every display, light fixture, and stock item in the store. All racks and fixtures were to be disassembled, cleaned, waxed, and polished. Then, each piece of merchandise was to be placed on the fixture in a specific order by size, style, color, and price. I couldn't believe it when I read that any fixture that supported merchandise on hangers had to be rubbed with wax paper so that the metal on the hangers didn't make a squeak when moved from side to side.

Normally, I would leave the store at 6:00 PM unless I was assigned to "close," but that first encounter with "The Great White Glove Edict" lasted until almost 10:00 PM. I had never been in the army, but I had no doubt that whoever came up with this plan was retired military.

It was overwhelming in scope and demanding in detail. I was suddenly terrified at the probability of humiliating failure. I spent several sleepless nights while the wheels of my imagination spun on the icy surface of 'White Glove Road.' I couldn't see how my group of tired, unmotivated "ladies" was going to get the required work done in less than two weeks. This was a 12-week project. I fantasized about getting in Jim's face and yelling as loud as I could, but all I could do was punch my pillow through the sleepless nights.

Finally, I reached the point where I didn't care if I failed. I decided to give it my best shot and to accept the consequences. I went to the store early the next morning, and I decided to try something I had read in a book by Dale Carnegie. I was going to find something to praise in everybody. I started with Mrs. Fullerton, who I found arranging the women's underwear.

"Good morning, Mrs. Fullerton, how are you this morning?"

"I'm fine, thank you," she replied politely. My "ladies" may have been old and slow, but they were very polite.

"You know, I don't think I've ever seen this section of the department look better! Very nice work, Mrs. Fullerton." Yes, I know that this sounds corny, but it wasn't flattery, and you should have seen the expression that dawned on Mrs. Fullerton's face. It was almost angelic!

I was so encouraged by the impact that this simple comment had on Mrs. Fullerton that I began to look for opportunities to praise and edify every one of my "ladies." The results were amazing.

That afternoon, I held a brief meeting on the daunting task of 'White Glove,' which was now less than two weeks away. I made a plea for their help. They knew everything about 'White Glove,' and I knew almost nothing.

Over the next two weeks leading up to the inspection, my troops went above and beyond the call of duty. I could not believe how hard they worked and the passion they had for the job. It was easy to find reasons to praise them, and the praise only spurred them to new heights.

Several of my "ladies" took on leadership roles during the frenzy to accomplish the impossible. A few even began to come in and work off the clock for free when I ran out of hours to assign. The much-maligned gaggle of middle-aged women whom Jim had often called "unreachable" had become a well-oiled machine of dedicated workers. It was magical, and it had happened almost overnight.

When the day of the White Glove Inspection arrived, each of my ladies stood like a proud soldier in front of her department. Doris Sharky came to our store early that day, prepared to defend us from criticism from upper management. She was shocked to find a gleaming store (as much as the Howling Street store could gleam anyway) full of smiling employees. They looked like little kids who had surprised their teacher with a particularly fine performance in the school play.

I didn't know whether to laugh or cry, so I did a little bit of both. I was incredibly proud of each of my "ladies" and what they had accomplished. The fact that they made me look good in the process was serendipitous. We received an excellent grade from all the managers that came through that day except one, and she was a malcontent who didn't give any of the 25 stores a high grade.

It would be another thirteen years before Walter would share his theory of human relations with me, but my experience with the ladies of Howling Street certainly confirms his theory.

Things really began to change the moment I began to see each one of the women in my store as competent, capable, skilled, qualified, and proficient. I think that the reason the result was so dramatic was the addition of praise and edification. The whole process was expedited because I didn't wait for them to "perceive" that I thought they were competent, capable, skilled, qualified, and proficient. I told them they were competent, capable, skilled, qualified, and proficient.

This open, honest (flattery would not have worked) and simple praise had edified them. I love the word "edification." In simple terms, it means "build-up."

Like most powerful ideas, edification is simple!

Can you imagine if everyone in the workplace began to look for competence in others and then used their discoveries to edify one another? Why not let the transformation begin with you? You can set the standard and lead your co-workers by example. You can bring about changes by uncovering the competence in others.

Chapter 5:
A Change in Attitude

After 4 years in the retail business, I started a new career selling surgical products with a company I'll call Surgical Devices. During my extended tenure with Surgical Devices, I have had the opportunity to work with a number of surgeons. In general, I am amazed by their skill, their patience, and their tireless devotion to their patients. Most people have no idea the sacrifices that surgeons make in their profession.

Let's just say that over the course of their careers, surgeons will get a lot less sleep than the rest of us. I have incredible respect for anyone who becomes a surgeon, and I am often dismayed when our society is so quick to blame them and sue them for not pulling a rabbit out of the hat every time.

There have been surgeons I have observed over the years, however, that I felt were not very **competent**. I mean no disrespect, but the reality is that not everyone who wields a scalpel is skilled and capable. Dr. Ima Whiner was a key surgeon operating in one of my hospitals that I felt was **incompetent.** I liked her as a person, and I respected her for her dedication, but I could not commend her for her surgical skills.

In private conversations, when her name came up, my first thought was, ***Dr. Whiner? I wouldn't let her near me with anything sharp!***

This, of course, is the best way to determine what your attitude is about someone. What is the first thing that comes to mind when you think of that person? Do you think they are **capable, skilled, qualified, and competent?** If not, then ***Walter's Theory*** predicts that you probably don't have a very good relationship with them.

This was certainly the case with my experiences with Dr. Whiner. It seemed like every time she operated, I received a bag full of bloodied, broken equipment labeled as "defective." Subsequent investigations by our quality team almost always pointed to "user error."

Dr. Whiner had a habit of forcing equipment past the breaking point on a weekly basis. It just seemed that although she was intelligent and personable, she lacked the hand-eye coordination and skill set necessary to be a good surgeon. While my opinions about her may have been true, and they could be supported by fact, they resulted in exactly the type of head-on collision you would expect based on ***Walter's Theory.***

Over the years, Dr. Whiner seemed to be a consistent obstacle to my success at St. Elsewhere. I would have agreement from the majority of surgeons over the purchase of our latest and greatest widget, and Dr. Whiner would veto the project.

At one point, Dr. Whiner led a campaign to completely replace all our equipment at St. Elsewhere Hospital with a competitor's product. Had she been successful, the loss would have been devastating to my career as St. Elsewhere was a large, loyal, long-time customer. I could not understand the reason for Dr. Whiner's continued opposition until I attended that fateful New Year's Eve party. The first person I thought of when Walter articulated his theory was Dr. Whiner.

No wonder this woman was so difficult for me to work with. I thought she was incompetent. But what could I do about that? She was incompetent, and I couldn't simply fake it and fool her because (1) I don't believe in flattery and faking it, and (2) I was sure she would still perceive that I thought she was incompetent.

I wrestled with this problem for several months, but it seemed like I had hit the wall. What good was *Walter's Theory* if all it did was point out why my relationship with Dr. Whiner was destroying my business?

Then, one day, I had the opportunity to observe Dr. Whiner teaching a surgery resident to perform a very difficult and specialized procedure. She was amazing. Her knowledge of the procedure and her skill in guiding the resident were awe-inspiring!

Suddenly, the light went on in my head. Dr. Whiner was a very **competent, skilled,** and **capable** "professor of surgery!" I realized that I had been judging her by the wrong standard. I began to see her in an entirely new light.

When her name came up, my first thought was, ***She is an excellent surgery professor!***

I had stumbled on her area of expertise, and I had also figured out a way to utilize ***Walter's Theory*** to dramatically change my relationships for the better.

Within six months of my ***'attitude adjustment,'*** I noticed a profound change in my relationship with Dr. Whiner. She dropped her opposition to my initiatives, and she became a strong supporter of the partnership we were forging with St. Elsewhere. Dr. Whiner became Dr. Winner, and ours was a true win-win relationship.

We became teammates with the noble goal of providing the best healthcare technology to the patients at St. Elsewhere at the best possible price. In retrospect, it was almost miraculous the way things changed because of this practical application of ***Walter's Theory.*** Now, I knew beyond a doubt that I had received a truly valuable tool that I could consciously use to forge a strong bond with others.

A new corollary to *Walter's Theory* formed in my mind: ***"The Attitude Corollary, which states: 'If you can discover competence in another person and make that your habitual pattern of thought concerning them, your relationship with that person will be optimized.'"***

After this, I began to consider the broader implications of what I had learned. Could ***Walter's Theory and The Attitude Corollary*** be applied to all relationships? What about the marriage? Is it possible that the foundation of most marriage discord is based on one partner thinking that the other is **incompetent?**

I could just see the couple telling the marriage counselor that their spouse was lazy, inattentive, slovenly, self-centered, unfaithful, and just plain **incompetent.** It seems unlikely that any marriage could be solid if either partner thought the other was **incompetent.** The opposite must also be true! Couples that had good marriages probably viewed their spouses as competent.

Applying the ***Attitude Corollary***, a wife could improve her relationship with her husband simply by focusing her thoughts (and her speech) on those areas where he is the most competent, i.e., ***"He works hard, and he's a good provider."***

It seems that the only time that ***Walter's Theory and the Attitude Corollary*** could not be applied with a positive effect would be in the case of an individual who is **totally incompetent.**

I suspect that very few people in the world fit this description, which means that there is a great deal of hope for the rest of us.

Chapter 6:
Double Vision

In every hospital, there is a materials manager or director of materials who is responsible for all the purchases of equipment and supplies that the hospital requires. Any sales representative who has ever attempted to sell any product to a hospital can attest to the fact that a good relationship with the materials manager makes life a lot easier, while a bad relationship with this person can make every day a struggle.

A few years back, I had a unique opportunity to observe a situation that reinforced my growing conviction that ***Walter's Theory*** might one day become known as ***Walter's Law.***

St. Elsewhere had just hired a new materials manager, Charles E. Buckmiser III. Chuck had transferred to St. Elsewhere from a nearby state hospital in another part of our region. His predecessor, George Wrath Sr., had been promoted, and most of the salespeople who had dealt with George were relieved to see him go.

My first meeting with Chuck was great. He had a good sense of humor and a good common-sense approach to business. He impressed me as being capable, experienced, and competent. I walked out of our meeting in very good spirits because I knew it was going to be a pleasure to work with Chuck Buckmiser. St. Elsewhere had become a very important account for me, and a good working relationship with Mr. Buckmiser would make my job a lot more fun.

One thing that Chuck had asked me to do for him in that first meeting was to put him in touch with Lester Slickman, the sales rep for one of our other divisions. I had impressed Chuck by sending Lester an e-mail before I even left his office. I followed up with a phone call to Lester a couple of days later because I felt that we were kind of chained together at the ankles in this account. If his division did not meet the customer's expectations, then it would definitely take some of the luster off my efforts.

When I got Lester on the phone, I was still excited about my first encounter with Chuck E Buckmiser. "Have you had a chance to talk with Chuck Buckmiser at St. Elsewhere yet?"

"I haven't actually talked with him yet, but I did leave him a couple of messages," Lester replied. "You met with him, didn't ya?"

"What'd ya think?"

"I really like this guy. I think he's going to be much easier to work with than George 'The Volcano' was!" I had been in the path of the verbal lava flow from more than one of Mr. Wrath's frequent eruptions. I wasn't sorry he'd been replaced.

"Ya, well, at least George had a backbone. I talked to some people who worked with Chuck at Pestilence General, and they said he was really weak when it came to supporting their contracts." Lester seemed pleased that he had garnished this piece of inside information out of the gossip gutter.

"Lester, that kind of thinking is going to get you in trouble. Did I ever tell you about *Walter's Theory*?"

"No, I don't think you did." Lester groaned. I could almost see him rolling his eyes on the other end of the line.

"Here it is in a nutshell. If you go in thinking this guy is weak and incompetent, you're going to make a very powerful enemy out of a potential ally. Trust me, Lester, it's dangerous to prejudge this guy's competence based on some rumor from Down South."

"Ya ya, I hear ya! Don't worry, I'll charm him," Lester crowed.

However, I was worried because I was beginning to believe very strongly that violating the principles of *Walter's Theory* would have far-reaching consequences. I suspected that Lester Slickman was about to add to the growing body of proof that *Walter's Theory* was, in fact, a **law.**

My suspicions were confirmed a week later when I ran into Charles E. Buckmiser III in the hallway at the hospital. At first, it was a pleasant encounter, but then he turned serious and expressed his severe disappointment that Lester Slickman had not been in to see him yet. It was very obvious that he felt disrespected and that he was angry about the snub. I assured him that I had spoken to Lester and that I knew he was trying to reach him. Charles was only slightly pacified, and I vowed to redouble my effort to see that Lester contacted him as soon as possible.

When I called Lester to encourage him to get in touch with Charles as soon as possible, he gave me a long list of assurances that he had everything covered. I tried hard to pop this bubble of self-confidence. "Lester, you need to get in and see this guy right away."

"Don't worry about it, man. This guy's not that important, anyway. I talked to some more people from his last job, and they all said he doesn't have the backbone to support us."

Now, I was really worried. "Lester, you can't afford to think that way about Chuck. Besides, I think you're wrong. He's already been a positive influence on me in a couple of situations."

I decided to plant a little seed based on *Walter's Theory.* "If you don't see him as competent and capable, Lester, he's going to pick up on your attitude, and your relationship with him is going to become a real problem."

"Like I said," Lester crowed, "you worry way too much."

Over the next several weeks, Charles used his influence to support our contract with the hospital. A prime example of how our partnership worked involved a sales rep named Fred Smeal from Outsider Enterprises. Fred was tall, imposing, and very pushy.

Apparently, his company made a gimmicky product that was considerably more expensive than my product, but Fred was really good at making unsupportable claims of product superiority. His favorite tactic was the hallway ambush. He would simply hang out in the hallways of the hospital and ambush surgeons in an aggressive attempt to get them to try his fantastic new product. There were several problems with this approach:

- First, the hospital already had a signed contract with my company to provide products that performed the same task reliably.
- Second, the hallway ambush was not only unprofessional but also violated the hospital's policy for vendors.
- Third, the majority of the claims of superior performance were simply not true.

- Fourth, the product and the complexity of its operation made it much more expensive.
- Fifth, Fred Smeal boldly lied about the costs, the performance, and the surgeon's support for his product.

I sat down with Charles Buckmiser to discuss this situation, and we came up with a plan to restrict the use of Fred's product to the few situations where it made sense and to deal with a product request that Fred was trying to push through the value analysis committee for additional items. I was to meet with the surgeons who were listed as "requesting surgeons" on the formal product request, and Charles agreed to meet with Fred to discuss his frequent violations of the hospital's vendor policy. It was a nice piece of teamwork that had a very positive result for my business and for the hospital's bottom line.

At the time we met, Fred had increased his annual business at St. Elsewhere to nearly $100,000. With the written request he was trying to push through the committee, this figure could have ballooned to over $300,000 in a very short time. That projected new business for Fred Smeal was coming right out of my pocket, and I was convinced, after reviewing the literature and talking with a number of surgeons, that the product he was hyping was inferior and more expensive.

As I began to execute my part of the plan, I learned that the surgeons listed on the written product request were not nearly as enthusiastic about bringing this technology into the hospital as Fred had said they were. In fact, several of them had little or no interest in the product.

Soon, it became apparent that Fred had filled out the product request form himself, including a number of misrepresentations. Several of the surgeons I saw called the nurses who represented them on the Valuation Committee to let them know their true sentiments.

A few days later, when the valuation committee met, the request for the additional products that Fred Smeal had been touting was **denied.** Charles Buckmiser III was the first to call me to tell me that he had personally recommended that the request be denied. I couldn't help but think how wrong Lester Slickman's assessment of Charles had been.

Within 3 months, hospital expenditures for Fred Smeal's line of products had dropped to **zero,** and Fred quit the company. The hospital saved over $40,000, and sales of my product rebounded to previous levels. Our partnership with the hospital grew stronger, and several other attempts by competitors to chip away at our business with St. Elsewhere were thwarted by Charles and I working together.

During the same period, Lester Slickman, surprised by the success we had achieved, changed his **attitude** about Charles. Within a very short time, Lester and Charles began working together to increase Lester's share of the business at St. Elsewhere. Without knowing it, Lester contributed to the growing body of evidence which showcases that ***Walter's Theory*** provides a valuable tool that can enhance business relationships.

Chapter 7:
The Platoon Blunder

The job with Surgical Devices was very high-pressure and very technical, but it turned out to be a good fit for me.

During my first five years with this company, I enjoyed considerable success, including a national award and a number of invitations to join the CEO at his home for dinner. It seemed that I had finally figured out what I wanted to be when I grew up.

Unfortunately, I still lacked wisdom in certain situations, and there were occasions when I said things that I would regret for years. One such occasion may provide useful insights as a practical proof of **_Walter's Theory._** I had been working for Surgical Devices for about 5 years at the time. I was on my way to our annual national sales meeting, which was being held in Tucson that year. Although it had been a very good year for me, our region had experienced a great deal of turnover. I had seen nearly 25 salespeople come and go during my tenure in our 8-man region.

The night before my flight to Tucson, I was watching the movie _Platoon_ with Charlie Sheen, Daniel Defoe, and Tom Berringer. There's a scene in the film that really grabbed me where one of the veterans of the *Platoon* tells one of the new replacements (he called them "new meats"), "Don't be surprised if I don't bother getting to know you for a while because you probably won't live that long."

The point was that the veterans didn't want to go through the emotional trauma of bonding with the replacements, who were often killed early in their tour due to lack of experience and training. It seemed like an exaggerated parallel to my experience with my co-workers. I had bonded with managers and other salespeople only to see them terminated in a few months.

The fact that I identified with this parallel so strongly led me to one of the more regrettable blunders I have ever made in interpersonal communication. I was riding in a town car from the Tuscon Airport to the Hotel with two other people. The tall, slender woman sitting next to me stuck out her hand and said, "Hi, I'm Annette Passionetti. I'm the new salesperson in Seattle."

I swear all I could think of was that darn movie Platoon as I replied, "Please, don't be offended if I don't bother to get to know you until you've been around for a while. It's not that I'm trying to be rude, but I've seen a lot of new reps come and go in the past few years."

Of course, Annette had not seen *Platoon* recently, and she was not only offended by my comment but enraged. For the next 10 years, my insensitive greeting served as a powerful motivation for her as she worked passionately to prove to me that she was not just more "new meat." She was very successful, and she held a number of sales and management positions with Surgical Devices over the years.

My relationship with her remained chilly, and on more than one occasion, our interaction deteriorated from chilly to frosty and from frosty to icy. I tried to explain the context of my stupid comment over the years, but it never really changed our relationship. I began to realize my father was right when he said, "Stupidity is its own reward!"

Then came the call that would change everything. Surgical Device's vice president of sales called me personally to tell me that Annette Passionetti had been promoted to regional manager. Effective immediately, she would be my new boss! I returned the phone to its' cradle with numb resignation. I had now been working for this company for nearly 17 years, but I was sure my days were numbered. How long would it be before Annette found an excuse to fire me? I didn't think I'd last a year. I imagined that she must be plotting how to send me out on patrol in enemy territory at the "point" position where the mortality rate was the highest.

I called Annette later that day and congratulated her on her promotion, and I promised to do everything in my power to support her in her new role (and I was sincere in this). She was very positive and gracious in her reply that she looked forward to working with me (and in hindsight, I know that she was sincere in this also).

Five years have now passed since the day we made our pact to work together, and it has been fantastic. Annette is the best manager I have had in my 23 years with this company. She is incredibly positive and supportive. The amazing thing is that we have not had any disagreements over the past 5 years regarding the right course of action to take with our customers.

We are of the same mind to a degree that is both wonderful and a little frightening at the same time. We both feel we are missing out if we are forced to go more than a few days without time to chat. We are a powerful team for our company and our customers. If I call Annette with a problem and I lay out several possible solutions, we always agree on the best course of action after a little discussion.

This complete turnaround seems totally illogical, but on closer examination, it is perfectly consistent with ***Walter's Theory.*** During the first 10 years of our peer-to-peer relationship, Annette thought that I was viewing her as incompetent. Certainly, my opening remarks to her questioned her ability to succeed in this job. Her reaction and her burning motivation to prove me wrong illustrate how deeply wounded she felt when her **competency** was questioned.

The reason for the turnaround in our relationship is less obvious but still totally consistent with ***Walter's Theory.*** As Annette and I began to work together, she stopped seeing me as an obnoxious peer and began seeing me as her most productive subordinate. She began to view me as a very capable, competent member of her team.

For my part, I stopped seeing Annette as a peer who held a grudge way too long, and I began to see her as a highly capable, efficient, and competent manager. Evidence of our change in perspective is clearly illustrated by the words we use to describe each other.

When people ask me about Annette, the first words out of my mouth are, "Annette is the best manager I have ever had, and I've had a lot of managers."

Whenever people ask Annette about me, I'm sure she tells them that she thinks I'm one of the best salespeople in the company. We definitely view each other as not just competent but very competent, highly effective, very skilled, extremely capable, etc.

As a result, we have a working relationship and a personal relationship that we both place tremendous value on. Although this relationship was built without either of us having any knowledge of ***Walter's Theory***, it definitely fits neatly the confines of ***Walter's Theory.***

Earlier this year, I also learned another interesting fact about Annette when we were at a regional meeting together.

She was addressing our group of 9 salespeople when she said, "I never bother telling you about your mistakes or the things that you have done wrong. I only focus on the things that you have done right and your successes. I know that each one of you is a highly motivated and capable salesperson. I also know that you realize when you make mistakes and that you will spend plenty of time beating yourselves up without my intervention."

No wonder we all think Annette is such a great manager. She demonstrates her complete faith in our **competence** by sparing us the "you should have done this and you should've done that" lectures. What a rare quality this is in a manager. Again, without knowing *Walter's Theory,* she is applying the main principle.

From this example, it becomes clear that *Walter's Theory* can be expanded to include managerial relationships with subordinates. Imagine what a pleasure it is to work for someone who does not bother to point out your mistakes because they view you as capable of self-correction.

Then, imagine that this same manager uses every opportunity available to give you accolades in front of your peers for your accomplishments. If you're a manager reading this, I challenge you to try this approach with your staff for one year. I'd be very surprised if you don't see a positive change in your relationship with your subordinates.

Chapter 8:
The Ragin Volcano

Any salesperson who has aspirations of selling anything from 10-cent band-aids to million-dollar robots to a hospital must first establish a relationship with the materials manager. The person in this position is responsible for obtaining the best products and the best service at the best price for his institution. It is a position that bestows a considerable mantle of power on the individual who sits behind the desk.

Over the course of my career, I have had considerable experience with a number of hospital materials managers. In general, I have great respect for them. They work long, hard hours, during which they must separate a constant stream of information from competing salespeople into two categories: FACT or FICTION. This is often difficult work that can lead to cynicism or worse. My experience with one materials manager is a prime example of the "or worse" individual.

My first encounter with Roger Raginfeller was harmless enough. Roger had just been promoted to materials manager at a Plague Valley Hospital. PVH had been a fairly good customer of ours for the past few years, but it had only recently been assigned to my territory.

Roger's office was really a Dilbert-like cubical open on one side to two other cubicles that were occupied by subordinates. It was actually the perfect killing field for the unwary sales representative, and Roger knew how to set up the machine guns for the most effective crossfire.

That first day, I introduced myself to the round-faced, pudgy-bodied man; I almost made the mistake of assuming that he was a rollie-pollie jolly guy who would be a lot of fun to work with. It didn't take me long to realize that this guy had little respect for salespeople. In his opening monologue, he made it very clear that he thought all salespeople were deceptive and dishonest.

His speech included a number of commandments, warnings, and threats and was delivered at a volume that was uncomfortably close to the threshold of pain. I wasn't really intimidated because I had been with Surgical Devices for over 15 years, and I prided myself on my honesty and professionalism.

At the end of Roger's opening remarks, I assured him that I would not give him any cause to "throw me out" of Plague Valley. Then came his first service request. The hospital had some special-order product that had not been delivered yet, and Rog wanted me to find out when it was going to come in. I told him that I would have an answer the next day and asked him if there was anything else I could do for him.

"No, just find out where my order is!" he bellowed.

As soon as I was out of the hospital, I put in a call to our customer service department on the East Coast. My customer service specialist told me that the product in question was on backorder but was scheduled to ship out the following Monday. I called Roger back and relayed the ship date I had been given. He seemed satisfied, and he asked me to check on the order again later in the week. I agreed.

When I called again on Friday, I was told that due to supplier delays, the order would not ship out until the following Thursday. I called Roger to tell him about the additional delay, and our conversation went something like this.

"Hello, Roger? This is Jay with Surgical Devices. I wanted to give you a call to let you know that your order has been delayed and that it will probably ship out Thursday instead of Monday."

Roger's reply took me totally by surprise. "You liar! You lied to me! You told me that my order would ship out on Monday, you damn liar!"

I'd known this guy one week, and already he was yelling the worst kind of accusation at me. It was ridiculous.

I decided that if I cowered and took this kind of abuse, the pattern would be established, and I could only expect worse treatment in the future.

"Roger, you don't know me that well, but you need to know this about me. I don't allow anybody to talk to me like that: not my manager, not the CEO of my company, and not any of my customers. I am not a liar, and I didn't lie to you. I gave you the best information available at the time. That information has changed, but that doesn't make me a liar."

I was shaking as I delivered my little speech. It was very tempting to give Roger an ultimatum or to threaten him, but I decided against it.

There was a brief silence on the other end of the line followed by some closing mumbling to the effect of "It better not happen again."

I wish I could say that standing up to Roger Raginfeller that first week had solved all my problems and led to a mutually respectful business relationship, but unfortunately, it was only 30 seconds into the first round of a 7-year boxing match. At least, it was the only time Roger called me a liar.

On a good day, Roger was a smoldering volcano venting sulfur-laden steam that burned your eyes and seared your skin. On a bad day, full eruptions of molten lava curses spewed from his tomato-red pudgy face. He was totally unpredictable, and to make matters worse, he routinely requested difficult, if not impossible, terms and concessions.

Nearly everything Roger asked required exceptions to company policy. Because I had been with Surgical Devices for over 15 years, I was usually successful in obtaining policy exceptions to accommodate Roger's whims. When I was successful, I dared not expect gratitude, and when I was unsuccessful, I could expect a barrage of curses, personal insults, and threats to give the business to a competitor. Despite all this, I got along with Roger better than most sales reps who called on him.

Over the course of our 7 years together, I was rewarded with dramatic sales increases with his hospital. It certainly wasn't because Rog liked me or because we hit it off.

In fact, about three years into our relationship, an incident took place that nearly destroyed everything. Roger had ordered a custom special-order instrument from us that was going to take at least 90 days to manufacture and ship. I was very careful not to promise a specific delivery date for fear of an eruption.

One day, in the course of a normal review of our business, he asked me about the special order. I had been anticipating the question, so I gave him the answer with confidence.

"Roger, when I called on your special order yesterday. I learned that it will not be shipped until mid-January because the plant where it is being fabricated is located in Sheffield, England. The plant will be closed in December because the English take the entire month off for 'Holiday.'"

Roger's face turned red, and the veins bulged near his temples and forehead. The whites of his eyes grew large, but the pupils became black holes. Without a moment's hesitation, he pushed the office chair he was sitting in across the room to where I was sitting, and he kicked me in the shin! I could not believe it. I stood up immediately, but I was too stunned to react. The two young trainees who were working with me that day just stared at me, wondering what I would do next.

I came very close to stomping out of the office and requesting an audience with Roger's boss, Rosemary. I had a great deal of respect for her, and I knew she would not approve of Roger's childish reaction. I could tell by the look on Roger's face that he knew he had crossed the line, but there was still plenty of rage in his countenance. I just stood there for what seemed like a very long time, weighing my options. Finally, I realized that more harm than good would result if I complained about this little episode.

As I look back on it now, I realize it was the right decision. In fact, I remember thinking at the time that I would have my revenge when I sat down to write my memoirs someday. Roger never apologized or even mentioned the incident, but I knew that he realized that my decision to keep it between us had saved him a considerable amount of grief.

Over the next four years, my business there grew dramatically, not because of any favoritism Roger showed me but in spite of him. I really didn't like Roger, and Roger really didn't like me. Roger really didn't like or respect any of the salespeople who called on him.

Roger always used to say, "You know how I can tell if a sales rep is lying to me? Their lips move."

Roger is the perfect example of why all those answers I gave to Walter's question on New Year's Eve and all the answers countless salespeople have given me over the years were WRONG. Roger's personality precluded nearly everyone from having a good relationship with him.

There was one thing about Roger, however, that I kept foremost in my mind. Roger was very competent. I often said that Roger never left any money on the table. He was a tireless negotiator for his institution. His loyalty to Plague Valley Hospital was legendary. It was this fierce loyalty that allowed him to justify his shabby treatment of salespeople. He was doing everything he could to squeeze the last nickel out of all the companies he had dealings with.

Knowing this, I chose to focus on his competency rather than his personality. I believe the fact that I viewed Roger as very skillful, efficient, and competent is the single most significant reason that I was able to work with him and grow my business with his hospital over a 7-year period.

The case of Roger Raginfeller not only serves to confirm ***Walter's Theory*** but also seems to suggest an interesting corollary. It seems that ***Walter's Theory*** provides an effective way to deal with difficult people. It may even be true that the more difficult the person, the more effectively ***Walter's Theory*** can be applied.

Just imagine how much better things might be for us if we looked for areas where difficult people are competent instead of concentrating our attention on how difficult they are to get along with!?

Chapter 9:
Stapling the NG Tube

During my career in medical device sales, I had parallel experiences involving two different surgeons. Both incidents involved a serious error committed during gastric bypass surgery. In this procedure, the stomach of patients suffering from obesity is divided with a surgical stapler to create a much smaller gastric pouch.

To aid in the procedure, a small clear plastic tube, called an NG tube (nasogastric), is passed down the nose into the stomach by the anesthesiologist. The tube is used to remove gas from the stomach and to help define the size of the pouch. It is a good idea for the surgeon to have the anesthesiologist remove the NG tube from the stomach before dividing the stomach with a surgical stapler. I was providing technical support for one of these cases with Dr. John Ponytail when he began to complain that our company's stapler was very difficult to fire. He continued to squeeze the handle, which emitted loud popping sounds like breaking plastic.

Dr. Ponytail cursed my product as he proceeded to open the jaws of the instrument. The complaining stopped when he realized that he had incorporated the NG tube in the jaws of the stapler, cutting and stapling the stomach and NG tube together. Only silence followed as he began to repair the damage that he had done. I was careful not to embarrass him further in front of his surgical team, but it was clear that the stapler was not the problem. I must admit that at that moment, it was difficult for me not to think of Dr. Ponytail as incompetent.

Shortly after that unfortunate incident, Dr. Ponytail led a spirited movement to have all our products at the hospital replaced with our competitor's products. Later, the account was assigned to a new territory, and it was no longer my headache or my **responsibility, but** I spent more than one sleepless night wondering what I could have done differently.

About three years later, I was working with Dr. Wonderkind, a very skilled young surgeon in my territory. He was also performing a gastric bypass surgery when he made the same mistake. He had forgotten to tell the anesthesiologist to pull back the NG tube, and he had inadvertently stapled it into the stomach. He was very upset with himself as he took the time to repair the damage.

At no time did he attempt to blame the stapler for the mishap. I immediately thought back to my experience with Dr. Ponytail, and I assured Dr. Wonderkind that I had seen this type of miscalculation before. In fact, I reasoned that every surgeon who performed this procedure had stapled the NG tube at least once.

Despite the fact that I had seen Dr. Wonderkind commit the same surgical error as Dr. Ponytail, I felt that Dr. Wonderkind was a much more competent surgeon than Dr. Ponytail. I continued to work with Dr. Wonderkind for a number of years, and the incident with the NG tube never had a negative impact on our relationship.

Two years later, my manager called me to ask me what I knew about Dr. Ponytail. I told her all the details of my experience with him, and then I asked her why the sudden interest in him. She said that Dr. Ponytail had contacted her and admitted to a number of technical problems with our competitors' products. He even admitted that perhaps he had been hasty in his decision to convert all products to our competitors several years before.

I was kind of excited at the prospect of recapturing the business at the hospital. I actually liked Dr. Ponytail personally, and I was looking forward to the opportunity to renew a relationship with him. I realized, though, that the fact that I had seen him commit a major surgical blunder might present a problem. I discussed this openly with my manager, and she resolved to meet with Dr. Ponytail to determine if he would be comfortable working with me again.

Several days later, she called me back to inform me that Dr. Ponytail was not willing to have me serve as his representative. Without being specific, he had told her that he had had problems with me as his representative. I was not surprised, but I was a little hurt because I knew that I had done a good job for Dr. Ponytail and his hospital during my tenure.

As I look back now in light of what I know about ***Walter's Theory,*** I can't help but wonder if the fact that I viewed Dr. Ponytail as less competent than Dr. Wonderkind had anything to do with the difference in outcomes I experienced with the two surgeons. The circumstances were nearly identical, but the final results were worlds apart!

Chapter 10:
Walter's Theory vs. Walter's Law

The first thing that I have to admit as a person with respect for science is that I can't say I have really proven that *Walter's Theory* should be reclassified as *Walter's Law*. What I can say is that the evidence I have gathered from my own experience seems to support *Walter's Theory*.

My hope is that by applying the principles of this theory, you will discover, as I have, that it can be the "Golden Key" to unlocking the potential in all your interpersonal relationships. I have no doubt that if you begin to look for the ways in which other people are competent, their perception of you will change and have a positive impact on your interactions with them.

In this book, I have focused on some of the business relationships that I had throughout my career. I believe very strongly that the same theory applies to all personal relationships, including friendships and marriages.

At the very least, I hope that the content of this book has started the wheels in your mind spinning in a new direction. Nothing would gratify me more than to hear your stories on the positive impact that *Walter's Theory* has had on your circumstances. Maybe together, we can prove that *Walter's Theory* is, in fact, *Walter's Law!*